THE 30-MINUTE BIBLE
READING AND DISCUSSION GUIDE

Maravillas Press
San Antonio, Texas

ISBNs: Paperback: 979-8-218-56285-4
eBook: 979-8-218-56286-1

Black and white illustrations by Martin Erspamer OSB
Cover and book design by Chris Tobias and Mayfly book design
Cover image: Christ and the Eucharist (illustration): permission to use image given by Brother Erspamer

Library of Congress Catalog Number: 2024925234
First Printing: 2025

THE
30-MINUTE
BIBLE

GOD'S STORY FOR EVERYONE

PAIGE P. VANOSKY WITH MATTHEW DAVIS

CONTENTS

ACT I: CREATION—GOD ESTABLISHES HIS KINGDOM

ACT II: REBELLION—SIN DAMAGES THE KINGDOM

ACT III: SALVATION INITIATED—GOD BEGINS TO RESTORE THE WORLD

ACT IV: SALVATION AND RESTORATION—GOD SENDS HIS SON, JESUS

ACT V: THE CHURCH—THE NEWS OF JESUS SPREADS

ACT VI: GOD'S KINGDOM ESTABLISHED FOREVER— JESUS' RETURN

---

* Chapter numbers of The 30-Minute Bible: God's Story for Everyone.

PREFACE

THE BIBLE IS A STORY of relationship. From the days of Adam and Eve in the Garden, we find God has sought to connect with His people. His desire to interact with all humanity is evidenced throughout the first couple's descendants until taking a dramatic turn with Abraham. It is through a particular line of Abraham's descendants, the Jewish people, that God begins a special relationship foundational to the overarching story. The important promises he makes to them will eventually turn back to include all the people of the world. Through this story, we catch a glimpse of who God is and how His story intersects with ours. As we do, we find the Bible is more than just an ancient text. It's the story of God reaching out to humanity, inviting us into a relationship with Him.

This story of relationship with God is deep and multifaceted, providing a foundation from which we can find answers to life's questions, such as:

* How can I find hope and peace?
* Does my life have a purpose? If so, how can I discover it?
* Is the God of the Old Testament angry? Is the God of the New Testament loving?
* Can God forgive me?
* How can I forgive myself and others?

To help readers understand the grand overarching story and, through it, discover answers to life's questions, *The 30-Minute Bible: God's Story for Everyone* provides an entry point. While it doesn't cover every book of the Bible, it highlights the major movements of God's story—a story whose depth surprises even those most familiar with Scripture. It is through understanding and reflecting on this big-picture story that we find help addressing our deepest questions.

This guide uses *The 30-Minute Bible* and *the Bible* itself to ask questions that enhance reflection and understanding. Please know that while this guide can be used by individuals, the richest insights often emerge from conversations with others. Sharing our thoughts and hearing others share theirs allows us to uncover truths that we might miss on our own.

So, grab a friend—or several—and perhaps a cup of coffee, and let's explore this remarkable story together, one often referred to as the greatest story ever told. We believe this journey will provoke thought, stir conversation, and deepen your understanding of God and His story.

P.S. Be sure to check out the Discussion Guidelines on the following page. These guidelines will help ensure that your conversations are enjoyable and fruitful, strengthening your relationships along the way.

GROUP DISCUSSION REMINDERS

Please keep these reminders in mind as you share your thoughts and listen to others share theirs during your time together. These are not rules, but principles that will help ensure a rich and respectful conversation for everyone.

> *"There are only a few things we need to agree on*—one day. Everything else is an interesting conversation."*
> —Rev. Dr. Buckner Fanning

* **Dome of Silence:** What is shared in the group, stays in the group. Respect others' privacy by not sharing their views or beliefs by name outside of this setting. The more trust you build, the more meaningful your discussions will be.
* **Respect Others' Opinions:** Listen with patience and curiosity. Differences of opinion are not something to avoid—they're opportunities to grow. You might even find yourself rethinking your perspective after hearing from someone else.
* **Treat Others as You Wish to be Treated:** Extend kindness just as you hope to receive it. Approach each conversation with empathy and understanding.

* **Agree to Disagree:** It's okay if we don't all share the same views. What matters is maintaining respect for each other, even when our opinions differ.
* **Focus on the Essentials:** Remember, the core of our faith unites us. Everything else is an invitation to explore and learn from one another.
* **Lead with Grace:** Approach every conversation with a spirit of grace. Mistakes, misunderstandings, and differing views are part of the journey. Give each other room to grow.
* **Be Brief:** As you share your thoughts, keep them concise to allow time for everyone to contribute. This will make the conversation more engaging and meaningful for all.

If we all follow these principles, our time together will be a meaningful experience of discussion and growth.

---

* **The Apostles Creed:** I believe in God, the Father almighty, Creator of heaven and earth, and in Jesus Christ, his only Son, our Lord, who was conceived by the Holy Spirit, born of the Virgin Mary, suffered under Pontius Pilate, was crucified, died and was buried; he descended into hell; on the third day he rose again from the dead; he ascended into heaven, and is seated at the right hand of God the Father almighty; from there he will come to judge the living and the dead. I believe in the Holy Spirit, the holy catholic Church, the communion of saints, the forgiveness of sins, the resurrection of the body, and life everlasting. Amen.

A WORD ABOUT BIBLE TRANSLATIONS

It's common to wonder about the different translations of the Bible, especially when considering which one to read. Questions often arise about who translated them, how reliable they are, and which one might be the best for your study. These are important questions, so we want to offer some clarity as you begin your journey.

First, it's important to know that most modern translations of the Bible are based on the original languages: Hebrew (for the Old Testament), Greek (for the New Testament), and some portions in Aramaic. But before the Bible was ever written down, it was passed along orally, with stories and teachings memorized and shared by word of mouth. Over time, those words were written on stone tablets and later on parchment. The Bible's journey from oral tradition to written form spanned many centuries.

Today, we live in a remarkable time when the Bible is more accessible than ever. It's available in many formats—large print, braille, digital versions on our phones—and we are close to seeing the Bible translated into every language on earth. The ease with which we can engage with Scripture today is a privilege, but it also raises the question: Which translation should I choose?

There are two main approaches to Bible translation: *word-for-word* and *thought-for-thought*.

* **Word-for-word translations** (also called "formal equivalence") aim to stay as close as possible to the structure
  and wording of the original text. These include versions
  like the **English Standard Version (ESV)** and **New
  American Standard Bible (NASB)**. They are great for
  in-depth study and understanding the specific wording
  of the original languages.
* **Thought-for-thought translations** (also called "dynamic
  equivalence") focus on conveying the meaning and message of the original text in a way that's easier to read and
  understand. Examples include the **New International
  Version (NIV)** and **New Living Translation (NLT)**.
  These are excellent for everyday reading and grasping the
  overall meaning of the text.

Some translations, like the **New Revised Standard Version
(NRSV)**, aim to balance these two approaches, offering both
accuracy and readability.

With so many translations available, it's important to
choose the one that best suits your needs. For casual reading
and group discussions, modern translations like the **New
Living Translation (NLT)** or **New International Version
(NIV)** are highly recommended for their clarity and ease
of understanding. For deeper study, word-for-word translations may be helpful if you're interested in the finer details
of language.

Another aspect to consider is the *resources* that come
with some Bibles. Some versions offer just the biblical text,

while others include helpful study tools like maps, footnotes, cross-references, and study guides. These features can enhance your understanding of the historical and cultural context of the passages you're reading or help you compare similar texts found throughout the Bible.

In the end, the most important thing to remember is that the best Bible translation is the one you will actually read. Whether you choose a word-for-word translation for study or a thought-for-thought translation for ease of reading, the goal is to engage with God's Word regularly. Many bookstores and online retailers carry a wide variety of Bibles, including different translations, resource options, and font sizes, so take the time to find one that works best for you.

THE BIBLICAL FAMILY TREE

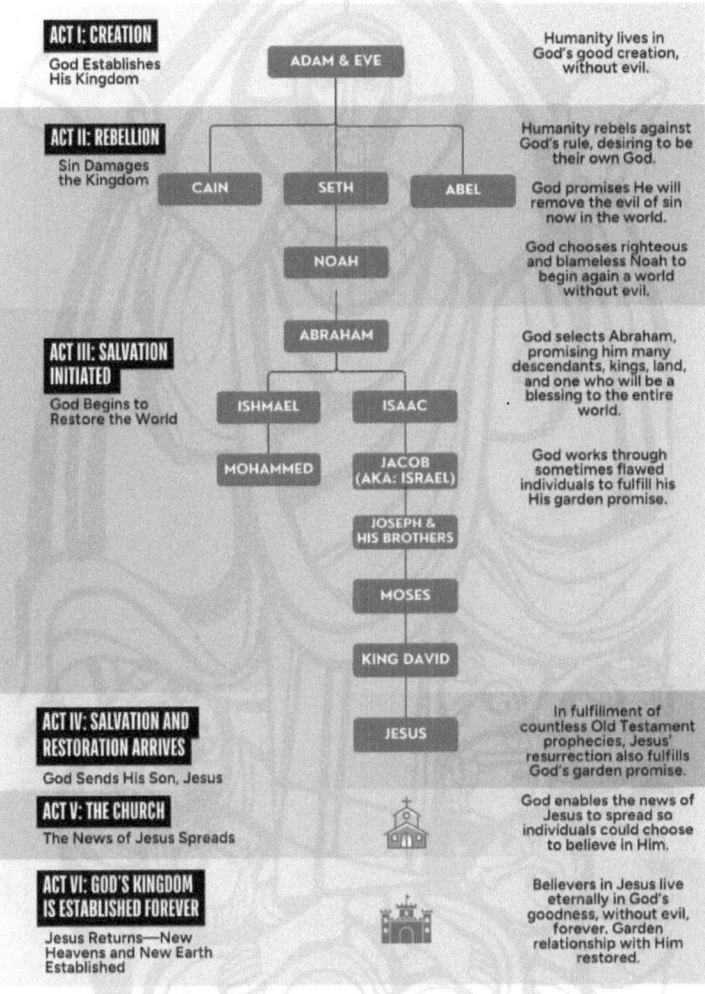

ACT I: CREATION
God Establishes His Kingdom

ADAM & EVE

Humanity lives in God's good creation, without evil.

ACT II: REBELLION
Sin Damages the Kingdom

CAIN — **SETH** — **ABEL**

Humanity rebels against God's rule, desiring to be their own God.

God promises He will remove the evil of sin now in the world.

NOAH

God chooses righteous and blameless Noah to begin again a world without evil.

ABRAHAM

ACT III: SALVATION INITIATED
God Begins to Restore the World

ISHMAEL — **ISAAC**

God selects Abraham, promising him many descendants, kings, land, and one who will be a blessing to the entire world.

MOHAMMED — **JACOB (AKA: ISRAEL)**

God works through sometimes flawed individuals to fulfill his His garden promise.

JOSEPH & HIS BROTHERS

MOSES

KING DAVID

ACT IV: SALVATION AND RESTORATION ARRIVES
God Sends His Son, Jesus

JESUS

In fulfillment of countless Old Testament prophecies, Jesus' resurrection also fulfills God's garden promise.

ACT V: THE CHURCH
The News of Jesus Spreads

God enables the news of Jesus to spread so individuals could choose to believe in Him.

ACT VI: GOD'S KINGDOM IS ESTABLISHED FOREVER
Jesus Returns—New Heavens and New Earth Established

Believers in Jesus live eternally in God's goodness, without evil, forever. Garden relationship with Him restored.

The 30-Minute Bible: God's Story for Everyone

ACT I:

CREATION:
GOD ESTABLISHES HIS KINGDOM

MEETING 1:
THE BIBLE AND GOD

T HE FIRST PART OF THE BIBLE, called the Old Testament by Christians and the Tanakh by Jews, is a sacred text to both Christians and Jews. It covers the beginning of the world and the history of the Jewish people. The second part of the Bible, the New Testament, focuses on Jesus' life and teachings. Christians believe Jesus is the fulfillment of Old Testament prophecies of a coming Savior.

God is seen as the ultimate author of both Testaments, inspiring forty human writers over 1400 years to write the stories found there. What makes these combined stories particularly remarkable is that each writer contributes to the same overarching story, using consistent themes that carry from the Old Testament into the New.

A "testament" is a covenant, or promise, between two parties. The Old Testament is centered around the covenant between God and the Jewish people, while the New Testament replaces that covenant with a New Covenant through Jesus.

This New Covenant is God's covenant promise extended to all people in the world. Whereas the Old Covenant was based upon law, the New Testament is based upon belief in Jesus as the fulfillment of the law. This is because His sacrifice was the ultimate and final sacrifice for the redemption of our sins—our failures before God. As we explore the Bible, we will discover how these covenants shape the biblical narrative and our understanding of God.

KEY TAKEAWAY:

The Old and New Testaments serve as the foundation of Christian faith. Together, they are called the Bible, a story inspired by God for everyone throughout the world. This story not only provides answers to life's biggest questions, but it also reveals God's nature and His commitment to a relationship with humanity throughout time.

DISCUSSION QUESTIONS:

CHAPTER 1: THE BIBLE
READ: 2 Timothy 3:16; Hebrews 4:12

1. **Inspiration for the Bible** The Bible is said to have been inspired by God for all humanity. How do you believe God inspired these words to be written? If you believe God inspires today, how?

2. **Trust in the Bible** Some people trust the Bible without question because of their relationship with God, while others seek evidence for its reliability. How do you approach this, and what helps you trust in Scripture?

3. **Understanding the Bible** Some view the Bible as entirely literal, while others see certain parts as allegorical. If the message remains the same, can we agree to disagree on this matter? Why or why not?

4. **The Bible and History** *The 30-Minute Bible* claims the Bible is the story of the world (page 9). As you look at the Bible's historical timeline on page 11, how do you see world history reflected in the Bible's narrative?

5. **Our place in the Bible** If the Bible is the story of the world, which act of that story do you think we are living in now? Provide your thoughts.

6. **Items for Clarification** Do you have any questions about the terminology or ideas presented in Chapter 1? Discuss any uncertainties you may have.

CHAPTER 2: CREATION
READ: Genesis 1:1–2:3

1. **God's Description of Himself** How would you describe God's character based on the creation story in Genesis 1? What aspects of His nature stand out to you?

2. **Higher Power vs. Creator God** Could the description of God in Genesis 1 be compared to modern ideas of a "Higher Power" or "The Universe"? What are the similarities and differences?

3. **First Audience Perspective** The book suggests that we should first view biblical stories through the eyes of the original audience before applying them to today. Do you agree with this approach? Why or why not?

4. **Factual or Allegorical** Whether you believe the creation story is factual or allegorical, does that change the overall message of the story for you? If so, how?

5. **A Changing Creation** Do you think a dynamic and ever-changing world could have been part of God's original creation plan? Why or why not?

ACT II:

REBELLION—
SIN DAMAGES THE KINGDOM

MEETING 2:
A CHANGED RELATIONSHIP WITH GOD

IN THESE EARLY CHAPTERS of Genesis, we explore the beginnings of humanity and our relationship with God. The stories of Adam and Eve, Cain and Abel, and the events leading to the flood offer insights into God's character and how He responds to sin.

These first eleven chapters of Genesis are considered "pre-history," stories passed down by oral tradition and later written under divine inspiration. In them, we begin to see God's purpose for creating humanity: to reflect His image, to care for His creation, and to live in relationship with Him.

However, sin quickly enters the picture, fracturing that relationship.

Despite humanity's rebellion, God surprisingly responds with grace and mercy, even as He judges sin. We see this in the way He provides for Adam and Eve after their disobedience and in His protection of Cain after the first murder. As we explore these stories, we can reflect on our own relationship with God and the consequences of sin in our lives.

KEY TAKEAWAY:

God created humanity for a relationship with Him, but our rebellion against Him results in separation. God's continual response with both judgment and mercy reveals His ongoing desire for a relationship with us.

DISCUSSION QUESTIONS:

CHAPTER 3: ADAM AND EVE—WHY ARE WE HERE?
READ: Psalm 8; Genesis 1:26-30

1. **Humanity in God's Image** How does humanity represent the image of God? What does this enable in our relationship with God that other creatures cannot experience?

2. **The Purpose of Humanity** What tasks did God give humanity in Genesis 1:26–30? Why do you think God gave humans these roles, and how do these tasks relate to our purpose today?

3. **Allegiance to God** If God created our existence, should we allow Him influence or direction in our lives? Do we have a responsibility to perform His will? Do you see the

Ten Commandments as an extension or clarification of
Gen. 1:26-20?

CHAPTER 4: REBELLION

READ: Genesis 3–4

1. **The Serpent's Deception** What was Eve's temptation
   (3:5-6)? This is known as the original sin. Are we tempted
   with believing the same thing today? What happens in
   our relationship with God that makes this a sin?

2. **Defining Sin** How would you define sin? How
   do you think this definition differs from modern
   interpretations?

3. **Before and After Sin** What was the relationship between
   the first couple and God before they sinned? How did it
   change after they disobeyed? How does this reflect in our
   relationships with God and with others when we rebel
   against a relationship with them?

4. **The Condition of the World** The image on page 28 of
   the book explains why the world is no longer the "very
   good" creation God intended. Do you agree or disagree
   with this explanation? Why?

CHAPTER 5: JUDGMENT AND MERCY

READ: Genesis 3-4; 6; 9:1-19; 11:1-9

1. **God's Response to Sin** Reread each story to see that God knew, He cared, He helped, He removed evil, He punished, He set them on a path to do better next time. Where do you find elements of grace or mercy in these actions? Are you surprised by any aspect of God's response?

2. **God's Foundational Promise** Summarize God's promise of Gen 3:15. Provide your thoughts as you compare this promise to Jesus' death and resurrection.

3. **The Flood and God's Desire** Why did God cause the flood yet save Noah and his family? What does this tell you about God's desire for humanity and the world He created? Do you believe this is still His desire today?

4. **The Tower of Babel** Do you believe the story of the Tower of Babel reflects rebellion against God just as Adam and Eve's disobedience does? Why or why not?

ACT III:

SALVATION INITIATED— GOD BEGINS TO RESTORE THE WORLD

MEETING 3:
ABRAHAM'S DESCENDANT WILL SAVE

IN THESE CHAPTERS, we witness God shift His focus to a specific person and family—Abraham and his descendants. God's promise to Abraham is pivotal, setting in motion His plan for redemption. Through Abraham, God begins to fulfill the promise of Genesis 3:15, addressing sin and starting a new chapter in His relationship with humanity.

What stands out is God's choice of Abraham—an old, childless, imperfect but humble man—to father a nation of God's people. Even more audacious is that God changes his name from *Abram* ("exalted father") to *Abraham* ("father of many") long before he has any children. This name change is not just symbolic—it is a bold declaration of God's promise to make Abraham the father of a great nation.

We also explore the stories of Jacob and Joseph, who, like Abraham, are imperfect but chosen by God to carry forward

His covenant. Their journeys are marked by struggle and transformation, showing us that God often shapes His people through adversity.

KEY TAKEAWAY:

The lives of Abraham, Jacob, and Joseph show us that God uses the weak, the flawed, and the overlooked to accomplish great things. Although Abraham and his descendants evidence doubt and are sometimes difficult, their story shines a light on God's faithfulness to His promises. As He walks with his people, He shapes them through adversity and enables them to become all that He calls them to be. We see that God remains faithful to His people and His promises throughout.

DISCUSSION QUESTIONS:

CHAPTER 6: GOD'S SOLUTION—ABRAHAM
READ: Genesis 12; 18:1-19; 22:1–18

1. **God's Promises to Abraham** List the promises God made to Abraham in Genesis 12:1–3 and Genesis 22:17–18. Using the Family Tree, can you begin to see how this story will unfold in the biblical story?

2. **Abraham's Doubts and Fears** What doubts and fears did Abraham express in Genesis 12 and 15? How do these moments of hesitation make Abraham's faith journey relatable to us today?

3. **Abraham's Righteousness** In Genesis 15:6, Abraham is called "righteous," in right standing with God, for his faith. Are you surprised by this? What does this reveal about how God views righteousness? Do you believe it is Abraham's head, hands, or heart that is most important to God? Why?

4. **Trust in Genesis 22 vs. Genesis 15** Compare Abraham's trust in God during the test of Isaac (Genesis 22) with his earlier struggles in Genesis 15. Do you see God shaping Abraham through these experiences? Do you see parallels in your life?

5. **The Testing of Abraham** Genesis 22 was an incredibly difficult test. How do you believe it helped Abraham durnig the long journey ahead?

Chapter 7: Jacob, Joseph, and His Brothers
READ: Genesis 28:10–22; 35:9–14; 45:1–28

1. **God's Choice of Jacob** Two common themese of the Old Testament are reflected in Jacob: God's selection of "the least of these", and God molding His people for great things. Do you believe God still molds us today to fulfill His plans, as He did with Jacob? Can you provide an example?

2. **Joseph's Trials** In your family, social, or work life, can you relate to the feelings Joseph must have felt during his years of betrayal and hardship?

3. **God's Involvement in Joseph's Life** In Genesis 45:58, Joseph recognizes God's hand in his life, even through the suffering he endured. How does this realization affect how you view difficult times in your own life? What insights or wisdom can you take from Joseph's story?

MEETING 4:
GOD RESCUES AND MOVES IN WITH HIS PEOPLE

THE JOURNEY OF THE Israelites, from slavery in Egypt to the foot of Mount Sinai, is one of God's most powerful acts of deliverance in the Bible. The story begins with God's call to Abraham, who, in trust, journeyed to Canaan, a land God promised to his descendants. Years after Abraham's arrival, a famine forced his family to Egypt where a descendant, Joseph, had miraculously risen to power and saved them. There they stayed for 400 years; however, by the end had grown in such numbers a new Pharaoh feared and eventually enslaved them.

Enter Moses, chosen by God to lead His people out of Egyptian slavery and into freedom. With God's help, Moses brought the Israelites to Mount Sinai where God made a covenant with His people, promising to bless them in return for their obedience to His laws. God's presence was tangible through their long journey, first through His presence in a cloud and fire guiding them. Later, God's presence came to reside in a tabernacle amongst His people.

KEY TAKEAWAY:

This magnificent story of God's love, forgiveness, and commitment to relationship is also evidence of God's grace, power, and omnipotence as we see Him providing for the needs of His people. In God's own timing, He rescues the people as a means to draw them to him, reminding them to be a light to others reflecting His love. He then provides laws calling for a loving relationship with Him, and a reverence of Him, as the basis for a godly relationship with others. These laws constitute an important covenant relationship between God and His people, the Old Testament Covenant, one with signs of a deeper connection to come.

DISCUSSION QUESTIONS:

CHAPTER 8: OUT OF EGYPT

READ: Exodus 1-7; 12; 14-15; 16

1. **God's Timing** In Genesis 15:12–16, God foretold that the Israelites would be in slavery for 400 years before He would rescue them. What was the reason for God's long delay? List all that you learn from this story.

2. **Moses** What do you learn from Moses and his changing relationship with God?

3. **God's Promise in Exodus** In Exodus 6:1–8, list the promies God gave the Israelites. What was the primary purpose God had for them? Think back to the creation story as you answer.

4. **Learning about God** Through these verses, what characteristics or insights do you find about God?

5. **The Significance of Passover** God instituted the annual Passover celebration to remember when death passed over the Israelites (Exodus 14:31–15:21). Which animal's blood on the doorpost saved them?

CHAPTER 9: MEETING WITH GOD
READ: Exodus 19–20

1. **God's Presence in Different Forms** What do you think God intended by manifesting His presence in the powerful ways He did on Mount Sinai? What does this say about God's knowledge of our needs and how we might experience His presence today?

2. **The Relevance of the Ten Commandments** Today, some think the Ten Commandments are outdated and no longer relevant. Yet, Jesus reaffirmed these commandments in Matthew 36:34-40. (Matthew 19:17; John 14:15-26, Matthew 22:36-40) If everyone in the world lived by these rules, what kind of world do you think we would have? Do you believe it would reflect the future world described in Revelation 21:4, where there is no more death, sorrow, or tears?

CHAPTER 10: GOD MOVES IN NEXT DOOR
READ: Exodus 24-34; 40

1. **The Old Covenant** In Exodus 19:1-8, and 24:3–8, we read that the Old Covenant is sealed with sacrificial blood. What is the Old Covenant i.e., what do God and the Israelites agree to with one another? This is the basis of the Old Testament, later to be replaced by the New Covenant of the New Testament. What do you believe the New Covenant is based upon?

2. **Encounters with God** Exodus 32-34 describes powerful encounters between God, Moses, and the Israelite leaders. What characteristics of God do you see revealed through these encounters?

3. **The Importance of the Tabernacle** God gave specific instructions for building the Tabernacle. Do you think these details were important to the Israelites or just to God? See also Hebrews 8 for your answer.

4. **God Dwelling among His People** Why did God choose to live among the Israelites, dwelling in the Tabernacle? What does this reveal about His desire for a relationship with His people?

MEETING 5:
GOD'S PEOPLE REJECT HIM AS KING

THE ISRAELITES WERE AT LAST on the edge of Canaan, the Promised Land, having completed their long and miraculous journey from slavery in Egypt. God had evidenced His awe-inspiring power and care for them during the journey, yet the Israelites did not trust that God would help them defeat the giants living in Canaan. They allowed fear to overtake their trust, and as a result, God declared they would not enter the land. Instead, He declared the next generation, one with deeper trust in Him, would be the ones to enter Canaan.

God instructed those entering Canaan to clear the land of its inhabitants. As harsh as it seems, this was rooted in God's continuing desire to establish His people in a land free from the evil practices of pagan worship. As the new generation of Israelites later entered the land, however, they failed to obey God and allowed pagan worship to infiltrate their lives. God sent judges and prophets to warn and guide them, but the Israelites continually turned their back on Him, eventually asking for a king like other nations. God granted their request, but the Israelites experienced the consequences. God then came to their aid, but they continually fell back, experiencing a repeated cycle of sin, punishment, repentance, and restoration from God.

KEY TAKEAWAY:

Despite all God had done for them, His people repeatedly struggled with trust and obedience. Yet, even when they rejected Him and asked for human kings, God remained faithful, offering guidance, leadership, and opportunities for repentance. What we discover is that without deep faith and trust in God, fear's grip becomes overwhelming to the point of disobedience, and terrible consequences result. Yet, because of God's grace and love, He is there offering restoration.

DISCUSSION QUESTIONS:

CHAPTER 11: THE LAND
READ: Numbers 13–14; Joshua 1; 24:1–28

1. **Characteristics of God in Numbers 13–14** After reading Numbers 13 and 14, what characteristics of God do you observe? How do these characteristics impact His relationship with the Israelites?

2. **God's Purpose for the Israelites in Canaan** What is the ultimate reason God sent the Israelites to live in Canaan (Deuteronomy 4:1-14)? How does this mission compare to the one Jesus later gives His followers in Matthew 5:14–16?

3. **The Ultimate Victor in Canaan** Joshua 5:13–15 reveals who would ultimately win the battle over Canaan. Who is it, and what do we learn from this?

CHAPTER 12: NO KING IN ISRAEL

READ: Judges 2:8-23; Judges 13-16; I Samuel 4:1-11; 7

1. **The Cycle of Sin and Restoration** The Israelites repeatedly fell into a cycle of sin, punishment, repentance, and restoration. Why did they fail and what was God's response? Have you experienced a similar cycle in your life, and if so, what has been the impact?

2. **"No King in Israel"** Judges 21:25 states that there was no king in Israel, and everyone did what was right in their own eyes. What king was missing—God or a human king? Does this speak to our individual lives or the global world today?

3. **Israel's Request for a King** God appointed Samuel, a godly man, as judge over Israel. When his sons proved unworthy, the Israelites asked for a king like other nations had (I Samuel 8:1–9). Why was it wrong for them to ask for a king? How did this point to a deeper issue in their relationship with God? Do you believe this reflects back on Adam and Eve and earlier stories?

CHAPTER 13: A KING LIKE OTHER NATIONS

READ: 1 Samuel 8:1-9:2; 16:1–13; 17:1–11, 32–50

1. **Saul's Characteristics** Saul was reluctant to become king. What were Saul's characteristics, and why do you believe God chose him (I Samuel 9:1—2)? Are Saul's qualities ones we often look for in those we choose to lead us?

2. **Saul's Trust in God** Although God changed Saul's heart (I Samuel 10:9–11), Saul's impatience showed his lack of trust in God (1 Samuel 13:1–14). What was the result of Saul's disobedience? Can you relate to impatience with God's timing?

3. **God's Silence to Saul** In the end, God stopped speaking to Saul (1 Samuel 28:15–19). What was the reason for God's silence? How did it affect Saul's leadership and relationship with God?

MEETING 6:
THE FAILURE OF HUMAN KINGS

THE ISRAELITES WISHED to be like the other nations, asking God for a human king. God, who was their true King, granted their request after warning them of the consequences. He provided three notable kings: Saul, David, and Solomon. Each king began with promise, but ultimately, all failed in different ways: Saul's lack of trust in God led to his downfall. David, though described as a man after God's own heart, committed serious sins that had devastating consequences. Solomon, known for his wisdom, fell into idolatry, leading to the division of the kingdom after his death.

KEY TAKEAWAY:

As the Israelites continue to deny God's involvement in their lives, God allows consequences to draw His people back to him. God answered the Israelites' request for a human king, giving them the best. As these kings ultimately fail the people, God's steadfast patience and commitment are evident through

His warnings, direction, and forgiveness. God is slowly unfolding His plan of redemption, laying the groundwork for what lies ahead.

DISCUSSION QUESTIONS:

CHAPTER 14: A KING AFTER GOD'S OWN HEART?
READ: 1 Samuel 16-17

1. **David's Qualities** What characteristic(s) did David possess that led God to choose him as king? (1 Samuel 16:7) How did David's faith and courage in the famous battle with Goliath reflect his heart for God?

2. **David's Sin and God's Response** After becoming king, David committed a grave sin with Bathsheba. How did God respond to David's sin (2 Samuel 12:1–23)?

3. **Why Did God Forgive David?** Despite his great sins, God forgave David. Why do you think God showed mercy to David (2 Samuel 12:13; Psalm 51; 1 Samuel 16:7)? What can we learn from this about repentance and forgiveness?

4. **Consequences of Sin** Although forgiven, David's actions had lasting consequences. How do you see the ripple effects of sin in individual lives or the world today?

5. **God's Plans for Solomon** David and Bathsheba's son, Solomon, was chosen for a special role. What were God's plans for Solomon as outlined in 2 Samuel 7?

CHAPTER 15: A WISE KING?

READ: 1 Kings 2:1–3; 3:1–15; 8:1–21; 11

1. **Solomon's Wisdom and Downfall** God granted Solomon great wisdom (1 Kings 3:1–15), yet after his death, the kingdom was divided. What was Solomon's ultimate downfall, and what lessons can we learn from his reign?

2. **Characteristics of Saul, David, and Solomon** Looking at the lives of Saul, David, and Solomon, what messages do you believe God is sending through these kings who started as godly leaders?

3. **Human Kings vs. God's Kingship** As you reflect on the kings of Israel and our country's leadership today, can God be our King although we live under human leadership? If so, how?

4. **God's Promise to Abraham** God promised Abraham descendants, a nation, kings, and a descendant that would bless the entire world. How many promises have been fulfilled so far in the story? How do these promises point to something greater to come?

MEETING 7:
UNFAITHFUL PEOPLE;
FAITHFUL GOD

SOLOMON'S REIGN, THOUGH marked by wisdom, power, and success, eventually led to division. The heavy demands he placed on his people resulted in the split of the united kingdom into the Northern Kingdom (Israel) and the Southern Kingdom (Judah). As both kingdoms began to stray from God toward pagan worship, they became vulnerable to neighboring emerging powers.

God, however, continued to speak to His people through prophets, offering both warnings and hope. The Israelites failed to listen, and the Northern Kingdom of Israel fell into idolatry under King Jeroboam. The Southern Kingdom of Judah, although maintaining temple worship, failed to live lives truly devoted to God. As a result, people from both kingdoms were conquered and exiled. We see God remaining ever faithful, providing promises of restoration and the hope of a coming Savior.

KEY TAKEAWAY:

Despite the Israelites' repeated unfaithfulness to God, He remains faithful to them. Through Israel's division, exile, and eventual return, we see the consequences of rejecting God. We also see, though, God's commitment to His promises and to His people. He never wavers, offering hope even in times of despair—the hope of a coming Savior.

DISCUSSION QUESTIONS:

CHAPTER 16: THE NORTHERN KINGDOM: ISRAEL
READ: 1 Kings 18:16–40; 2 Kings 17:1–18

1. **Idolatry in the Northern Kingdom** King Jeroboam led the people of the Northern Kingdom into worshiping the pagan god Baal. This shift from the worship of God to idolatry happened so easily. Does the same thing happen today? Discuss Sunday worship versus a personal, heartfelt worship of God and how to obtain the later.

2. **Ahab and Jezebel's Influence** King Ahab's marriage to a Baal worshiper, Jezebel, led to his downfall. Do you have relationships that take you from a stronger relationship with God? In contrast, what keeps you or others from straying from God and faith?

3. **God's Persistent Communication** Throughout Israel's history, God continued to speak to His people through judges, prophets, and demonstrations of power. What does this reveal about God's character? Do you believe God communicates to us similarly today? If so, how?

CHAPTER 17: THE SOUTHERN KINGDOM—JUDAH

READ: Jeremiah 7:1–14; 2 Kings 24:1–25:21

1. **Ignoring Warnings** Judah failed to heed the warnings of prophets like Jeremiah. As a consequence, the Babylonians destroyed the temple and took the people into captivity. Where was God during this time—was He forming them, or had He abandoned them? What can we learn as we face struggles today, corporately or individually?

CHAPTER 18: EXILE AND RETURN

READ: Psalm 137:1–6; Jeremiah 29:1–14; Jeremiah 31:31–34; Ezra 1:1–7; Haggai 1

1. **Despair in Exile, Hope in Promise** Psalm 137:1–6 captures the despair of the Israelites in exile. Have you ever felt such despair, or do you feel it now? As you read Jeremiah 29:10–14, how does the hope found in these verses speak to you today? What characteristic(s) of God do we find in Jeremiah's words?

2. **God's Promises through the Prophets** Isaiah and Jeremiah both prophesied that after seventy years in captivity, the Israelites would return to their land (Isaiah 48, Jeremiah 29:1-14). Do you see God's faithfulness in fulfilling these prophecies? What encouragement does this offer us in difficult times?

3. **The Coming Savior** Through the prophets, God also spoke of a coming Savior (Isaiah 52:13–53:12;). What do these passages teach you about the coming Savior, and how does it compare with what you know of Jesus?

4. **The New Covenant** Jeremiah 31:31–34 speaks of a New Covenant, one that will be different from the Old Covenant. What is this New Covenant, and how does it change the relationship between God and His people?

CHAPTER 19: AN IN-BETWEEN TIME
READ: Isaiah 40; Mark 1:1–8

1. **Different Views, One Plan** During this period, many Israelite sects formed, each claiming to have the correct understanding of God's plan. Yet none got it right. What should we learn from this about differing prophetic interpretations today?

2. **History and the Bible's Validity** How do you view biblical stories as you read historical events interwoven into them? Does it affect the validity of the Bible for you?

3. **God becomes Silent** The Israelites must have wondered where God was when He suddenly became silent during their 400 years in captivity. Can you relate to their feelings? How does Isaiah 40 offer comfort and hope for those who wait on the Lord?

ACT IV:

SALVATION AND RESTORATION—GOD SENDS HIS SON, JESUS

MEETING 8:
ABRAHAM'S DESCENDANT—
THE SAVIOR

THE ISRAELITES HAD NOT HEARD from God
for 400 years until, suddenly, a voice crying in the wilderness broke the silence. It was John the Baptist. Quoting Isaiah 40:3-5, he began calling for repentance and preparation for the coming Messiah, telling the people to prepare for the King's arrival. Surprisingly, though, he meant to prepare their hearts, not their roads.

One day, he was preaching when a humble man from Nazareth came forward for baptism. John immediately recognized Him, announcing to all He was the Promised Savior. As Jesus was baptized, God's voice from heaven called Jesus His Son, and the symbol of the Holy Spirit, a dove, descended upon Him. Once empowered by the Spirit, Jesus' public ministry could begin. Jesus came as God's answer to humanity's deepest need, offering salvation to all who would believe in Him.

KEY TAKEAWAY:

After centuries of waiting and silence for God to fulfill His garden promise, God sent the promised Savior. Born to an impoverished and scorned couple, the Savior represented "the least of these." However, born in the line of Abraham and King David, Jesus' arrival, life, death, and resurrection would fulfill many Old Testament prophecies, bringing salvation for *all people* who believed.

DISCUSSION QUESTIONS:

CHAPTER 20: A VOICE CRYING IN THE WILDERNESS

READ: Luke 1:5–25, 57–80; John 1; Matthew 3

1. **The Birth of John the Baptist** Continuing an Old Testament theme, God worked through an old, barren woman to bring about the birth of John the Baptist. God used John, not a noted individual, to introduce the Messiah to the world. Provide your thoughts.

2. **The Importance of Repentance** John the Baptist and Jesus both preached repentance (Mark 1:15). What does true repentance entail, and why do you think it's so central to the message of the Bible? Do you remember times when we've seen God seeking repentance in the Old Testament? Do you believe it is important to our faith today, and if so, why?

3. **Evidence of Repentance** John challenged the crowd to show evidence of repentance in their lives (Matthew 3:7–10). What causes a person to repent, and how is it evidenced in an individual's life?

4. **The Meaning of Baptism** What does baptism represent in the life of a believer and in our relationship with God?

CHAPTER 21: THE ONE
READ: Luke 2

1. **The Angel's Message to Mary and Joseph** Imagine being Mary or Joseph. A virgin couple learning Mary would bear a Son they were to call "He Saves" (Jesus). How do you think they processed this, especially knowing Jesus would be both God's Son and a descendant of Abraham, Jacob, and David?

2. **Fulfilled Prophecies** Discuss some of the prophecies fulfilled by Jesus' birth:
   * He shall be called Mighty God." (Isaiah 9:6–7)
   * He will come from a virgin birth. (Isaiah 7:14)
   * He will be despised and rejected. (Isaiah 53:3; Luke 4:28–29)
   * He will enable the blind to see. (Isaiah 35:5–6; Matthew 11:2–6)

   ✳ They will cast lots for His clothing. (Psalm 22:18; John 19:23–24)

   ✳ He will be abandoned. (Psalm 31:11; Mark 14:50)

What do these prophecies teach us about God and His plan to restore our relationship with Him?

3. **Jesus' Early Life** Most of our knowledge about Jesus' younger years comes from Luke 2:22–52. What insights do these passages provide about Jesus' upbringing and His understanding of His identity?

4. **Jesus as the Ultimate Way to God** Remembering God saved the Israelites so that he could bring them to himself (Exodus 19:3-6), do you see Jesus as God's new way to save and bring individuals to Him? (Acts 3:25b; Luke 24:47; John 17:23)

CHAPTER 22: JESUS BEGINS HIS PUBLIC LIFE

READ: Matthew 3:13–4:11, 18–22

1. **The Trinity at Jesus' Baptism** At Jesus' baptism, we see the Father, Son, and Holy Spirit together. Discuss your understanding of the Trinity and how you perceive the relationship between the Father, Son, and Holy Spirit.

2. **The Power of the Holy Spirit** The Holy Spirit played a significant role in the lives of John the Baptist, Mary, and Jesus. How do you see the Spirit's power at work in these stories, and how do you think the Holy Spirit continues to work in the lives of believers today?

3. **Jesus' Selection of the Twelve Disciples** What is surprising about the men Jesus selected to be His disciples. How do these choices connect to Old Testament themes, and what does it signify about Jesus' mission? How does this speak to us today?

MEETING 9:
JESUS—FORGIVENESS, HEALING, AND HOPE

JESUS' PUBLIC MINISTRY BEGAN when He was around thirty years old and lasted for just three short years. Yet in that brief time, His teachings and actions profoundly changed lives, then as now. People marveled at His wisdom and authority, as He taught not like the religious leaders of the day but instead as one who spoke with the authority of God Himself. Some even accused Him of blasphemy as He claimed to be one with the Father and the source of eternal life.

Jesus lived a life that reflected God's perfect love. Through miraculous healings and compassionate interactions with the marginalized, He fulfilled what God had asked of Israel but that they did not do—embody God's love for the world and, in so doing, reflect God's image in the world. Jesus' arrival was the beginning of God's Kingdom on earth, and He promised that one day, He would return to fully establish that Kingdom.

KEY TAKEAWAY:

Jesus changed the course of history in just three years. Through His teachings and miraculous healings, He brought the good news of the arrival of God's Kingdom of love, offering hope and healing to all who would believe in Him. Jesus became the way to a new and eternal relationship with God. It is now belief in Jesus as God's Son and the Promised Savior, belief in His life, death, and resurrection that saves. Through this belief, we develop a heartfelt desire to live Godly lives, and, as we have seen throughout the Old Testament, God looks to the heart. This is the New Covenant God offers in the New Testament through Jesus. The Old Covenant of the law has been replaced by belief in the one who fulfills the law, whose death as the final unblemished lamb offers atonement, Jesus.

DISCUSSION QUESTIONS:

CHAPTER 23: WHAT JESUS TAUGHT

READ: Mark 1:14–45; Matthew 13:18–23

1. **The New Covenant** Jesus announced the good news of a New Covenant between God and humanity. Under the Old Covenant, the people had to follow God's laws to be part of God's family. Under the New Covenant, however, faith in Jesus as one's personal Savior is all that is needed. Summarize the following verses speaking about this: Matthew 26:27-29; Romans 10:4; Hebrews 8; John 3:16; Romans 5:1-2

2. **Jesus as the Sacrifice** Old Testament covenants were sealed with blood offerings. As the blood of the lamb on the Israelite's doorposts saved them from death, providing life in their escape from Egypt, so Christ's blood as the final Passover lamb provides eternal life to believers. (Hebrews 9:11-28). Discuss.

3. **Jesus' Second Coming** Jesus promised to return one day (Matthew 24; John 14). Why do you think God planned for two comings of Jesus? How does this align with what we've seen of God's character in the Bible?

4. **The Parable of the Sower** In Matthew 13:18–23, Jesus uses the Parable of the Sower as a means for us to consider the type of soil we have in our hearts for God's Word. Spend time reflecting on this. If you feel your soil could be improved, what steps might help recondition it?

5. **The Power of Faith** In Matthew 17:20, Jesus speaks of the power of even the smallest amount of faith. What do you think it means to have faith like a mustard seed? What does this thoughtful statement tell you about Jesus?

CHAPTER 24: WHAT JESUS DID

READ: John 1:29–34; Luke 23

1. **The Miraculous Healings of Jesus** Read the healing accounts in Mark 1:21–45, 4:35–41, and John 11:1–44, listing the various types of infirmities Jesus healed. What do these miracles tell you about God's Kingdom on earth?

2. **Jesus' Approach to Healing and Compassion** Reflect on Jesus' actions and approach toward the people He encountered in these stories. How did He treat those in need, and what does this teach us about how we should approach people in need today? (John 4)

3. **The Light of God** Do you see a connection between God's stated Old Testament desire for people to reflect Him in their lives (made in His image, purpose of entering Canaan, etc.), and Jesus' commandments to follow Him? Provide your thoughts.

4. **Living like Jesus** Jesus was a "light on the hill," showing the world what life with God truly looks like. As Christians, we are called to live like Jesus. Do you see this happening in the world today? If you are a Christian, is this something you are striving for in your own life? What does it take to "strive"? Discuss.

MEETING 10:
GOD VICTORIOUS OVER EVIL

JESUS' LIFE, DEATH, AND RESURRECTION were the culmination of God's plan to defeat evil and restore humanity to Himself. Throughout His ministry, Jesus fulfilled prophecies, healed the sick, and taught with unparalleled authority. But as Jesus began claiming to be the Son of God, the political and religious leaders felt threatened. Ultimately, it was the people of Israel who demanded His crucifixion, unable to reconcile His humble beginnings with the idea of a Savior.

Importantly, we note that Jesus willingly went to Jerusalem despite knowing what awaited Him. In an act of perfect sacrifice, He was willingly crucified during the Passover, the commemorative time God commanded the Israelites to remember when the blood of a lamb had saved them from death in Egypt. Through Jesus' death on the cross, He became the final unblemished lamb, offering eternal life to all who believe. But the story didn't end with His death. Three days later, Jesus rose from the dead, appearing to His disciples and countless others over the next forty days, solidifying the truth of His resurrection and His victory over evil.

KEY TAKEAWAY:

Through His death and resurrection, Jesus triumphed over sin and death and fulfilled countless Old Testament prophecies of the coming Savior. Now sitting at the right hand of God, His resurrection provides the foundation of Christian faith, offering hope and eternal life to all who believe.

DISCUSSION QUESTIONS:

CHAPTER 25: FATAL CONFRONTATION

READ: John 1:29–34; Luke 23

1. **Jesus' Willingness to Die** Jesus told His disciples what would happen to him when they reached Jerusalem (Mark 10:32-34), yet He willingly went. What does this tell you about Jesus' willingness, and how do you feel about the disciples, His friends, fleeing in fear for their lives when He was arrested? (Mark 14:12-50)

2. **The Lamb of God and Passover** As the introduction to Jesus' ministry, John the Baptist called Jesus "the Lamb of God who takes away the sin of the world." Reflect on the symbolism of Jesus' crucifixion happening during

Passover, when the blood of a lamb allowed death to pass over the Israelites. How does Jesus, the final unblemished lamb, allow death to pass over us? (Luke 22:7–38)

3. **The Verdict on Jesus** What conclusions did the Chief Priest and Jewish leaders reach about Jesus (Matthew 26:57–66)? What did Pilate and Herod conclude about Him, and why did the people call for His crucifixion (Luke 23:1-25)?

4. **Jesus' Words from the Cross** While on the cross, Jesus said, "Father, forgive them, for they do not know what they are doing" (Luke 23:34). How should His words influence our thoughts toward those who crucified Him and, by extension, those who wrong us?

5. **The Importance of Jesus' Humanity** Jesus' humanity is evident in His final moments on the cross (Mark 15:34). Why is it significant that Jesus experienced human suffering and death? How does this affect our understanding of Him as our Savior (Luke 22:42; John 16:33)?

6. **Jesus' Compassion on the Cross** In Luke 23:38–43, Jesus responds to the criminal's faith in Him. What does this interaction teach you about Jesus' heart for the lost, even

in His final moments? What does this tell us about what it takes to be saved to eternal life?

7. **If This Were the End** If the story ended with Jesus' death, what would we think of Him today? Discuss what His death would have meant without the resurrection.

CHAPTER 26: ON THE THIRD DAY
READ: Luke 24; Acts 1:6–11

1. **Jesus' Response to Doubt** How did Jesus respond to those who needed physical evidence to believe in His resurrection? How does this encourage or challenge your own doubts?

2. **The Importance of the Resurrection** Many believe in Jesus' life and death but stop short of believing in His resurrection. Why is it essential to believe that Jesus rose from the dead? What are your thoughts or doubts? Discuss the significance of the resurrection in your faith.

3. **Jesus' Response to His Fearful Disciples** How did Jesus respond to the disciples who had fled in fear during His arrest and crucifixion? What can we learn from Jesus' grace toward His followers?

4. **Understanding Scripture after the Resurrection**
   During Jesus' post-resurrection appearance to His disciples, He explained the Scriptures concerning Himself (Luke 24:45–49). What do you think He might have said, and how would that have deepened the disciples' understanding of Him?

5. **Fulfillment of God's Promises** God fulfilled His promises to Abraham, Isaac, and Jacob by providing descendants, a land, and kings. The final promise to be fulfilled was that one of their descendants would bless the entire world. How does Jesus fulfill this promise through His life, death, and resurrection? How is Jesus' resurrection a crucial answer to Genesis 3:15?

ACT V:

THE CHURCH—THE NEWS OF JESUS SPREADS

MEETING 11:
BELIEVING THE UNBELIEVABLE

AFTER JESUS' RESURRECTION, He spent forty days appearing to His disciples, preparing them for their mission to go into all the world, but commanding them to wait for the Holy Spirit to empower them. After Jesus' ascension, they were together when, suddenly, the Spirit arrived in a powerful way. They began speaking in different languages, able to communicate the gospel to people in all nations. This moment, Pentecost, marked the birth of the church.

The Apostle Paul had his own dramatic encounter with the risen Christ, leading him to become one of the most influential leaders of the early church. A former leading persecutor of Christians, his encounter with Jesus was life-changing. His missionary journeys and letters spread the gospel far and wide, establishing churches and mentoring believers in their faith. Empowered by the Spirit, the church grew despite the persecution of believers, proving that nothing could stop the message of Jesus.

KEY TAKEAWAY:

The birth of the church, fueled by the Holy Spirit, marked the beginning of the global mission to spread the gospel of Jesus Christ. This fulfilled prophecies from the garden (Gen. 3:15) and subsequent prophesies that God's family would one day include the whole world, not just the Jewish people. From Jerusalem to the ends of the earth, Jesus' followers overcame fear and persecution to share the good news. The Apostle Paul led the charge, establishing churches and writing letters that continue to inspire us today.

DISCUSSION QUESTIONS:

CHAPTER 27: THE CHURCH IS BORN
READ: Acts 2; Genesis 11:1–9

1. **The Importance of the Ascension** Jesus ascended into heaven. Imagine witnessing this event. Why is it important for us to believe in the ascension today? (Psalm 110:1; Luke 22:69; John 16)

2. **The Arrival of the Holy Spirit** At Pentecost, the Holy Spirit arrived with great power, allowing the disciples to speak in different languages (Acts 2:7–12). This moment reversed the division that began at the Tower of Babel (Genesis 11:1–9). What are your thoughts on this connection?

3. **Peter's Sermon** After the Spirit descended, Peter preached a powerful sermon explaining the Scriptures and pointing to Jesus as the fulfillment of prophecy (Acts 2). What thoughts or questions do you have about Peter's sermon?

4. **The Role of the Holy Spirit in Witnessing** Jesus told His disciples to wait for the Holy Spirit before sharing the gospel. Do you believe it is important to follow the leading of the Spirit when witnessing about Jesus today? How do you think Christians can allow the Spirit to lead them? (John 14:26; Matthew 28:19–20; Ephesians 4:30; 1 Corinthians 6:19–20)

CHAPTER 28: FROM JERUSALEM TO THE ENDS OF THE EARTH
READ: Acts 7:54–8:3; 9:1–31

1. **The Transformation of the Apostles** The apostles fled in fear when Jesus was arrested but later faced martyrdom spreading His message. What does this transformation tell you about the truth of Jesus and His resurrection?

2. **Paul's Radical Conversion** Saul, the chief persecutor of Christians, became its greatest evangelist after encountering Jesus (Acts 9; Acts 26). What about Jesus could have resulted in Paul's dramatic conversion? Does this

transformation testify to the truth of Jesus for you? Why or why not?

3. **The Early Church in Action** Acts 2:42–47 gives a beautiful picture of the early church, where believers shared everything in common and cared for one another. Do you see this happening in churches today? What would it take for churches to embody that level of love and care, and should they?

CHAPTER 29: PAUL—THE SENT ONE

READ: Acts 19; Philippians 1:1-2:11

1. **Faith and Reflection** After meeting Jesus, Paul believed, but also took time to reflect on prophecy (Galatians 1:11-24). Some people believe in Jesus immediately, while others need time to study and reflect. Which path resonates with you, and why?

2. **Paul's Preparation and Calling** Once empowered by the Spirit, Paul began his missionary journeys, courageously telling others what he now knows (Acts 13). Acts 19 provides insight into all that his continued travels accomplished. Provide your thoughts.

3. **God's Power over Evil** Despite persecution, the early church grew as people accepted Jesus as their Savior. What does this tell us about God's power over evil, and how does this encourage us in today's world?

4. **Paul's Words About Resurrection** In 1 Corinthians 15:20–22, Paul writes about the resurrection of the dead through Christ. As you think about this about this, describe your beliefs and hindrances to belief.

"But Christ really has been raised from death—the first one of all those who will be raised. Death comes to people because of what one man did. But now there is resurrection from death because of another man. I mean that in Adam all of us die. And in the same way, in Christ all of us will be made alive again. (1 Cor. 15:20–22)

ACT VI:

GOD'S KINGDOM ESTABLISHED FOREVER—JESUS RETURNS

MEETING 12:
HEAVEN ON EARTH FOREVER

THE BOOK OF REVELATION is biblically unique in that it speaks of the future—of a time when Jesus will come again to bring God's Kingdom to earth in its fullness. This is a time when everything will be made new, when God will dwell with His people, and when sorrow and suffering will cease. The entire biblical narrative points toward this moment of final victory. Satan will be crushed by Jesus once and for all.

God's consistent desire to dwell with His people is evidenced throughout the Bible. It is seen in the Garden of Eden, the Tabernacle, the coming of Jesus, and ultimately, in the new heaven and new earth. The Bible's story is our story, one that invites us to live in relationship with God now and for eternity.

KEY TAKEAWAY:

The final chapters of Revelation reveal God's ultimate plan—a new heaven and a new earth where He will dwell with His people forever. This eternal Kingdom brings an end to sorrow, suffering, and death, fulfilling all of God's promises and establishing the fullness of life in Him.

DISCUSSION QUESTIONS:

CHAPTER 30: END THAT IS NO END
READ: Revelation 11:15–19; 21:1–8; 22:1–6

1. **The Vision of God's Kingdom** Revelation paints a picture of what the world will be like when God's Kingdom is fully established on earth. From what you've read, how do you envision this future? What do you think life will look like in this new heaven and new earth?

2. **Fullness of Life Today vs. the Future** Jesus promised fullness of life to His followers. Do you believe this fullness can be experienced in a believer's life today, or do you think it is something that will only come with the arrival of God's Kingdom on earth? (Philippians 4:12)

3. **Fulfillment of God's Promises** In Genesis 3:15, God promised that Eve's offspring would defeat Satan.

Throughout the Bible, it was also prophesied that a descendant of Abraham and David would bless the entire world. Is it difficult to believe Jesus is the fulfillment of these promises? Why or why not?

4. **God Dwelling among His People** Revelation 21:1–4 tells us that God will dwell among His people once again, saying, "They will be His people, and God will be their God." Discuss the significance of this phrase, and reflect on other times in the Bible when when God has made this promise. (Exodus 6:7; Ezekiel 36:24-28)

5. **The Bible as Our Story** As we look at the consistency of the biblical story, with so many authors over so many years, and the way history intertwines with the narrative, do you believe the Bible is the story of our world? Do you feel that you are a part of this ongoing story? If so, where are you in the story?

6. **A New Heaven and a New Earth** Revelation speaks of a time when there will be no more sorrow or suffering. As you read about this new creation, describe what you envision.

THE BIBLE: SUMMARY QUESTIONS

1. **Your Understanding of the Bible** What has struck you the most about the Bible and the biblical story as we've journeyed through it together?

2. **Your Understanding of God** Has your understanding or description of God changed during this journey? If so, how?

3. **Strengthening of Faith** Have you come to a new understanding of the Bible? If so, has it strengthened your belief in Jesus, God, or the truth of the Bible? If so, in what ways? What do you still struggle with?

4. **Recurring Themes** As you reflect on our discussions, what biblical themes have stood out to you? Have you noticed consistent themes about God, Jesus, the Holy Spirit, or humanity? Have you noticed God's timing, patience, forgiveness with repentance, or other key themes?

5. **Jesus as a Blessing to the World** Consider that Jesus came to be a blessing to the entire world, not just to a specific denomination or faith group. What thoughts or

questions does this raise for you, and what are the implications for how we relate to those of other faiths?

6. **The Essential Tenets of Faith** Looking back at the Essential Tenets of Faith we discussed in the first meetings, has your faith grown in any of these areas? Do you have a new understanding of the Apostles' Creed and its significance in your life?

EPILOGUE AND NEXT STEPS:
CONTINUING THE CONVERSATION

A S WE BRING THIS discussion guide to a close, it's important to remember what we've experienced together in this group. Believe it or not, what we've done here is *church*. Not church as many of us picture it today—with big buildings, bands, fancy lights, or particular music—but church as it originally was. In the early days, the people of God came together in small gatherings, just as we have, to talk about what God was up to in their lives—past, present, and future.

The early church wasn't perfect, and neither are we. The people of God throughout history have always been flawed, as we've seen throughout our study, yet God has remained faithful. Just as God didn't give up on His people then, He doesn't give up on us now. And we shouldn't give up either.

KEEP THE CONVERSATION GOING

We invite you to consider keeping this conversation going, either with this group, another group or by finding an entry point into a local church. Church doesn't have to be a big, formal gathering. It can be a small group of people who come together to talk about God's work in the world.

If there's one thing we've learned together, it's that faith is a journey, a journey of growing faith and trust. It's meant to be walked alongside others. The Bible says, "For where two or three gather in my name, there am I with them" (Matthew 18:20). God is present when we come together, just as He has been with us through these weeks. Whether with this group or another, find a way to keep discussing faith, asking questions, and sharing what God is doing in your life.

THE BIGGER PICTURE

Through our discussions, we've seen that all people are invited into the family of God. Paul writes in Galatians 3:23–29 that, before Jesus, we were held under the law, but now, through faith, we are all children of God. Whether Jew or Gentile, slave or free, male or female, we are all one in Christ Jesus. This unity in Christ means that we belong to something bigger than ourselves. We are heirs of the promises given to Abraham—promises of hope, forgiveness, and eternal life.

Galatians 3:23–29 reminds us of this unity: *"So in Christ Jesus, you are all children of God through faith ... there is neither Jew nor Gentile, neither slave nor free, nor is there male and female, for you are all one in Christ Jesus."*

JESUS: THE FULFILLMENT OF THE PROMISE

Throughout the Bible, we've seen that the law was given as a guardian until Christ came (Galatians 3:24). Jesus didn't come to abolish the law but to fulfill it (Matthew 5:17). What humanity couldn't achieve through obedience to the law, Jesus accomplished through His life, death, and resurrection (Romans 8:3–4). He is the promised descendant of Abraham through whom the whole world would be blessed.

Still, Abraham's family is large. As we read in Genesis, Abraham had two sons—Isaac, the child of the promise, and Ishmael. Both of these sons went on to father great nations, with Isaac's descendants forming the Jewish people and one of Ishmael's descendants the founder of Islam. The complexity of Abraham's family reminds us that God's promises stretch across nations and generations, and even today, those promises are alive in Jesus, the fulfillment of God's plan for all people. (John 3:17; Mark 16:15; Matthew 28:18–20)

WARNINGS AND HOPE

Throughout Scripture, God warns His people, urging them to turn from their ways. The prophet Isaiah spoke of "a great and terrible Day of the Lord" (Isaiah 13:6) if people didn't change their hearts. Despite the warnings, Israel often chose to ignore

God's call, leading to dire consequences. Do you believe we receive similar warnings today, and if so, do we avoid them like the people of Israel?

When we face troubles in our world today, it's easy to question God. But as we've seen throughout the biblical story, God is moving humankind into a world without evil. In the midst of Job's extreme sorrows (Job 38:1–40:42), God reminds Job of His power and sovereignty over all creation. When we think about the troubles of today, hopefully we can now endeavor to view the difficult aspects of life in light of God's ultimate power and plan.

ALIGNING OUR WILL WITH GOD'S

One of the most powerful lessons of this journey is that those who seek God's will for their lives will find their desires aligning with His. When we pursue God and trust in His plan, our lives take on a new direction—one that is guided by His Spirit and marked by purpose. In Romans 10:4, Paul reminds us that Christ is the end of the law for those who believe. As we've seen in the lives of Abraham, Isaac, Jacob, and Jesus, God's plan is perfect, even when it's not easy to understand.

FINAL THOUGHTS

We hope you know that each encounter with the Bible provides a new perspective. The insights never end—they continue in your life, in your relationships, and in your walk with God. Keep seeking, keep asking questions, and keep growing in faith.

The Bible evidences that God does not give up on His people, and He won't give up on you now. Keep the conversation with Him going as you keep walking with Him.

Remember to trust the process. God's people have never been perfect, and neither are we, but God remains faithful. Keep walking, keep growing, and keep trusting.

God is with you.

With all blessings,

Paige and Matt